44 POEMS FOR YOU

44 POEMS FOR YOU

SARAH RUHL

COPPER CANYON PRESS

PORT TOWNSEND, WASHINGTON

Cover art: Phil Kovacevich

Copper Canyon Press is in residence at Fort Worden State Park in Port Townsend, Washington, under the auspices of Centrum. Centrum is a gathering place for artists and creative thinkers from around the world, students of all ages and backgrounds, and audiences seeking extraordinary cultural enrichment.

LIBRARY OF CONGRESS CATALOGING-IN-PUBLICATION DATA
Names: Ruhl, Sarah, 1974– author.
Title: 44 poems for you / Sarah Ruhl.
Other titles: Forty-four poems for you
Description: Port Townsend, Washington : Copper Canyon Press, [2020]
Identifiers: LCCN 2019019608 | ISBN 9781556595844 (pbk. : alk. paper)
Classification: LCC PS3618.U48 A6 2020 | DDC 811/.6—dc23
LC record available at https://lccn.loc.gov/2019019608

9 8 7 6 5 4 3 2 FIRST PRINTING

COPPER CANYON PRESS
Post Office Box 271
Port Townsend, Washington 98368

www.coppercanyonpress.org

For Tony

Personism, a movement which I recently founded and which nobody knows about, interests me a great deal... It was founded by me after lunch with LeRoi Jones on August 27, 1959, a day in which I was in love with someone (not Roi, by the way, a blond). I went back to work and wrote a poem for this person. While I was writing it I was realizing that if I wanted to I could use the telephone instead of writing the poem, and so Personism was born. It's a very exciting movement which will undoubtedly have lots of adherents. It puts the poem squarely between the poet and the person, Lucky Pierre style, and the poem is correspondingly gratified. The poem is. . . between two persons instead of two pages.

Frank O'Hara

A gift that cannot be given away ceases to be a gift.

Lewis Hyde, *The Gift*

CONTENTS

I

II

III

IV

V

VI

VII

44 POEMS FOR YOU

I

I wanted music

I wanted music   yes

but I also wanted the music

of everyday things

a plate   an arm   some dirt   a chair

how a plant is related to a window

how a window is related to a chair

small words with purpose

correspondences

of everyday things

the music of combustible objects

one day ending

not tracking for posterity

but loosening like a fig

You made me soup

One made me laugh
one made me travel
one made me speak
one made me unravel

One made me quiet
one made me sad
one made me sing:
has have had had

But you made me bread
you made me soup
you made me sing:
honor the world.

Hope Street

arbor of skin
arbor of trees
arbor of stomach
arbor of knees

one unsaid name
one unsaid tree
one unsaid house
one unsaid sea

un said the house
un said the tree
un said my mouth
un   said   me.

Marginal questions for snowless children

was it ever snowing

        without snow
        in your childhood

did time turn
into snow

did snow turn
into time

what did you do
with a windowsill

did time ever slow

        on a snow day
        school bells
        ring for no one

        angels are
        in bed

        when families change
        their cadence
        tables get smaller

        all a child can
        do is wait for snow

can cold things
be merciful

        yes, I think they can

does a child
need snow
to instruct
the emotions
to learn
what falls
even without motivation

what is white
what is brown
what is grey

who told you
to sleep late
who told you
the world would wait
for your sleeping body
to absorb more indoor air
more snow follicles

for indoor grace
for outdoor coverings
for someone to say
the will is a landlocked rudder
boats don't go in snow
this morning is not for industry

how much silence

were you allowed

no snow

around your ears

Why are you so sturdy?

1

Why are you so sturdy?
You are:
a bed, a desk, a chair.

I am somewhere else.
Maybe in the air.

2

I like:
the look of broken springs
when they are sad and old.

You like:
for a thing to work—
a body, a stove, a string.

3

I long for the moon.
You're eating with a spoon.
The spoon works.
The moon looks up and down.
No work for the moon.
She wilts. Or glows.
Gets smaller. Or bigger.

The moon
has no truck
with the spoon:
silver, milk,
cereal, sky.

And what of love.

4

I would trade
a large and practical room
for a room
the size of a window
from which to see the moon.

I intend to give you many bowls

1

I intend to give you many bowls
for apples and loose change.

What would suit you
better than a bowl.

Round with primacy,
place for holding.

You are not round
like a woman
but you have more
roundness than most men.

2

In Korea,
every day a woman
prays for her son to come
home.

Every day she puts clear water
in a bowl.

She places it in the garden.

3

I will deposit light when you're absent.
Figs. Water. Unchurched compounds.
Tithes and dithyrambs. Light.

4

A bowl.

Where a mother
puts a son for safekeeping.

Fugue on the
preeminence of corners.

Cornerstone
of repeated silence.

Something to eat
and light is changing.

A bowl:

Two cupped hands
made of clay.

Why even speak of it

1. why even speak of it

because you were willing to be silly

2. a bargain

teach me words for fixing
bodily harm. I will teach you
your childhood starting with:
a yellow rain slicker.

3. where did this take place

bench, brown church, pink house, garden

4. a prayer to be said over the unscientific weary:

I bless thee, temporomandibular joint
I bless thee, buccal artery and nerve
I bless thee, depressor anguli oris
I bless thee, zygomatic arch
I bless thee, temporal fascia

what happens when a man or boy
says this blessing over an unhappy
girl or woman in a garden

5. a few more prayers

a prayer for boats
a prayer for coincidence
a prayer for tailors
a prayer for sleep
a prayer for windows
that they might be open

a prayer for thinking
up suitable prayers

6. why even speak of it

because you said:
write me a happy poem
on the occasion of my sadness.

I will praise your plain songs

I will praise your plain songs.
I will praise your plant songs.
You will give me weeds
and distraught calendars.

I will praise you for the things you choose:
the color of your shirts.
I will praise you for unchosen things:
the contour of your chin.

You will give me subscriptions, brevity,
towers of flat, sweet grass.
You will give me pointed flower arrangements.

When summer flags and ships slow
and I am tired of waiting, tired of praising
bits and pieces, thumbs and drawers—anatomy—
then I will praise you without purpose,
your empty hands, your hollow ear. . .

When your nothing things are incomplete
(when your nothing is complete)
the work of conspiring solitudes—
I will praise your nothing best and most of all,
I will praise you in the smallest, saddest words:
so, then, to, cup, go.

Addressed to the gods of unnecessary labors

Some say: to do the necessary task is greatness;
I say: do the least necessary thing first.

I don't want a frozen living room,
a room where nothing happens.

I don't want my labors tied in string,
a prelate hovering over, declaiming.

I want a treasure I did not ask for,
the way I didn't ask to be born.

I want your arms and legs to be happy;
I want my arms and legs to be warm.

I want us to lie there, while the sky overhead
vigorously, vigorously does nothing.

Prayer

Let the day open slow around you.
Let the night open slow around you.

Let the spring open slow
the fall open slow
the waking animals open their eyes slow
around you.

Let the night close slow around you.
Let the day close slow around you.

The winter close slow
the summer close slow
the sleeping animals close their eyes slow
around you.

II

Watching my father breathe

I have been watching
you breathe lately,
watching the little boy
pucker, as though you
are blowing bubbles in your sleep,
breath disturbing your entire frame,
now a bird's nest,
breath winding through your lungs and
through the forked canoe of your trachea.

You breathe a plate
of uneaten egg salad and tomatoes
up and down your middle
(she has been trying for
days now to feed you)
while you look outside—
"Look, the serviceberry tree has berries!"—
you cry, as though the triumph of the berry
could enter your body, as though
an army of berries could multiply
in your marrow, blotting out the cancer.

My mother consults books—
she wants to know where blood goes when it dies,
picking at scraps of knowledge
that the sparrows leave behind.

She never did believe in the body,
but she is learning now that the brain is
planted in the body the way
a bulb is planted in the earth; she is
learning to feed you and I am learning
to watch you breathe and we are all

learning the peach pit of the heart
and the day-old avocado of the liver and the
substance of breath in the body.

Driving to Iowa on Christmas Eve

to my sister

The last time we drove to Iowa
before my father died,
he and my mother sat in the front,
my sister and I in the back,
our heads rolling onto each other's shoulders,
our necks two stalks with buds too big for standing.

The warm car in the cold air looks out on
purple fields of snow-blanketed corn.
The night is the color of a lavender mussel—
and we are the fruit of enclosure—
a dark, soundless mussel, yards below water,
inside the walls of a domed shell.

My father looks straight into the road that
keeps replacing itself, looks at
the shadows of corn he used
to detassel in the summer, his innocent hands
helping the shy boy and girl corn to mate,
the sky as hot and golden as young corn in heat.

He drives straight into the vertebrae of the country,
straight into this Midwest with its prolonged childhood
and reams and reams of sky,
while his family tastes the last sleep drawn
from the comfort of this configuration,
this configuration of going home—

the father is driving,
the mother is in front,
the two sisters are in back,
sleeping.

Dressing

What do I wear in the morning
for the afternoon when you will die.
How will I take my leave of you:
in black, white, or in rose colors.

Do not rush down the slope of your going—
I am at my bureau
looking through shirts:
a red shirt stained with life,
a white shirt stained yellow,
button missing, safety-pinned, wrinkled.
It must not be black.
A brown dress for comfort?
A brown dress for the harvest that will not come?

My drawer is emptied on the bed.
Please wait for me to choose
the shirt, the shoes,
the hat, the tie—
please wait for me to dress
for the afternoon when you will die.

In Praise of Old Age

I envy men with wrinkles.
I envy men with canes.
I envy men with broken bones
and horrid, raised-up veins.

I envy men with hemorrhoids
and men with balding heads.
I envy men with bad toupees
who wish that they were dead.

I envy every grandfather
and every mark of age
that didn't get a chance
to draw its lines
upon your face.

Death in Another Country

I sometimes feel that I learned
death in another country,
a country prickling with
lace and dried grass.

A country in which the pews of churches
are filled with flowers bobbing their heads in song
and where the weeping women
rise mute from black bean soup.

Perhaps I learned death from the
country of children,
from my cousins searching for more
corpses to gaze at in the funeral parlor,
death interesting like an ant carrying a pebble
in its mandible, death strangely beautiful like
limbs moving slowly underwater.

I do not know what to do with my eyes,
how to meet the eyes of adults mourning,
or how to turn down the corners of my mouth.
I do not know how to arrange my hands.

I know only that I am far from that
shadowy region where death
paints his blue colors,
cast by trees at night.

I am still looking at the moon,
looking for my father.

Red Leaf

I would like to send this
tiny red leaf to you.

It is the size of a toenail
with yellow piping
down the center, ribbon
for the fine hair of baby birds.

For you to hear the sound of my throwing
this leaf to you, I would have to sound like
ten thousand canyons ripping apart or louder.

For you to see the yellow piping down the center
I would have to paint as bright and bold
as ten thousand suns or brighter.

For you to touch the leaf's veins,
subtle as the wrinkles under your eyes,
I would have to sculpt rivers as wide as planets
with all the earth's clay.

Perhaps all art is a
trying-to-send of a tiny red leaf
almost stepped on
to a deaf someone who
might not hear it.

Perhaps all art is
a hollow knocking
at the closed door
of the dead.

Driving to Iowa Two Years Later

This time, we drive into daylight,
the sun dodging us slightly,
though the road seems never to move.

Electrical sign-posts like sentries,
metal cobwebs, a tin woman with her
arms akimbo, a squat Eiffel Tower
with the thighs and hips of the Midwest.

The land knows starkly who's missing this year.
The air bitter, light-drenched, colder than snow.
Brown and white burs clutch the ground.

My sister sleeps beside me in the front seat.
I drive, the only noise the choke of tollway bumps,
reminders of slowness.

Signs for Dixon, Naperville, DeKalb, Peace Road.
White light on silos, the sun an ovum-shaped
cough drop disappearing.

There is nowhere for the sky to hide in the Midwest;
vastness cannot hide behind barns.
The sun, she can hide only a hangnail
behind silos, behind pigs.

Mother is in a separate car, mulling over the day's
events. I try to drive quietly so my sister will sleep on.
Soon we will go over the bridge, suspended by green girders,
soon our breath will be miles
above the Mississippi.

III

Block Island

You watch the ship
I watch you watch the ship

What is it you like
about the angle of distance?

Stalwart fragility
west wind
east wind
south wind. . .

Cormorants
sand divots
purple shadows in the sand
red bog
duck crossing
and the lighthouse
we pass in silence

Song

Lay your body down, my love,
Lay your body down.
I'll love you hot and white and brown.
Oh, lay your body down.

I'll play your ribs a harp, my love,
your chest a violin.
I'll sound out all the air inside
the hollow place within.

Your teeth a tinny triangle,
your mouth a golden lute.
Your toes quick, ugly eighth notes,
your ears the knobs of flutes.

I'll make your body sing, my sweet,
the praises due to love
until the wheeze of death
that blows in every lover's lungs.

That festive sad accordion
goes a-wheezing up and down,
Oh, lay your body down, my love,
Oh, lay your body down.

Song for hands on Thursday

Let me be forthright for the moment.
I want to speak simply for once:
I like your hands.

Your fingers don't act like I'm a lily
by a pond in complicated overtures of rain.
Your hands don't feel compelled
to sing the warbling discourse
of souls—Aquinas gestures, that sort of thing.
They don't say: your body is a far-off bird call
rounding up red-faced militia men
to their morning devotionals and ablutions.

Your hands are warm.
They've touched cadavers.
They know time is short for warmth.

This morning is a Thursday.
It is not a day for beginnings, endings,
or strategically placed middles.
It is a day to live—
a brown bowl, a warm carrot.

Tomorrow and tomorrow
are two funny men in bowler hats—
you can see their noses, their hats, and their overcoats—
they are reading the evening news—
the probabilities of horses, the longevities of pork.
Don't pay those two flunkies any mind.

Your eyes are those of a soft-spoken boy,
maybe eight years old,
walking through a yellow field in bare feet.

His feet retreating, then moving forward,
then, at last, he puts his shoes on,
his eyes retreating under their lids for sleep.

Twin Hip Bones

Twin hip bones,
Twin prime numbers,
A day will not always look like this.

You in the evening and you in the morning,
My hip bone curving, your hip bone curving toward mine.

A day will not always look like this,
You in the evening, and you in the morning.

Someone please describe to me the beauty
of asymmetry:
one hip bone, one number, one branch.

A day will not always look like this,
with you for beginnings and endings—
and for between: the long, yellow night.

Tithe

Supposing I loved you with simple grace
untoward, untried, with reversal of tithe—
unchurched meaning this: I would give nine-tenths
of my thoughts to you and one-tenth to the rest of the world.

Supposing the little earthenware jug in my chest
were to get full of practical things—
lamp here, lamp there, bread bread sleep.

IV

Father's Day

She learns to write,
surrounded by planets
and birds.

She of your cheeks
and your chin.

He learns to walk,
unsteady, his eye
unsteady too, like yours.

She learns to jump.
"Candleball!" She shouts
up into your arms.

Your arms—
as steady as your father's
arms were unsure.

She learns to swim the same
summer your mother learns to die,
with the same grace, the same sureness in becoming,
both acquiring an underwater knowledge.

Terrible summers come to an end,
and you, hands on your chin,
watch your three children,

becoming.

Anniversary

A little box of
days spent together, married.
What is it to be married.

Married is: a day
at Cora's café
you say, You're a good wife, am I a

good husband? Yes, I
say, then we swim. Married is:
we talk about our

bodies, you tell me
what's in your stomach and we
talk of itchy bumps.

Married is: you come
home, my eye is hurt, you come
fast and put

a warm towel on me.
And married is: Anna runs
between us, so much

joy on her face and
it is your face and it is
my face and it is

her face and she runs
and the smell of
apples in winter.

Ash Wednesday with Anna

At the playdate I thought I smelled strange.
Iron, or sweat. She screamed joy at a plane.
A man walked by with ash on his head.

"It's Ash Wednesday," I said. "I forgot this year.
Bad Catholic." We went home and I saw blood. I lost
her sister or her brother or maybe just

a sense of possibility while unloading groceries. It snowed
in March today. I fed her a cheese sandwich,
felt a strange pulling and yelled "Oh!" She, two
and a half, said "Thank God." I kept bleeding.

No one teaches how Jesus's blood cleaned him,
or how Mary bled for a month after birth.

There was blood in the hay and blood on the cross.
Beginnings and endings are marked with blood. What of middles?
Ash Wednesday, waiting mid-week, mid-body,
full stop in the middle of possibility.

Miscarriage

When I first said I was bleeding your face changed,
then we went on as before.
Watched comedies on television,
stuffed vegetables into the vegetable drawer.

It wasn't until you saw blood in the toilet,
saw the red unfurl, you let sadness in.
A doctor, you're used to seeing red on white.
You've seen what lives under skin.

Medical sadness waits upon sight;
mine, a mole, needs no light.
Every month women practice for this—
casual loss as a regular thing—

women bleed in private like animals,
men bleed in public like kings.

v

Poem for weary mothers

for Sherry Mason

What you don't imagine when you're pregnant:

The fevers, the falls, the nights without end.
How worry will become a placeholder for thought.

Pink medicine and nebulizers and the fight to
put on socks, cough drops buried in your purse
beside forgotten cheese.

How worry will become a companion,
like another heart, or lung.

And:

How nothing will ever smell as good as your
boy's hair when the sunlight hits it.

Mothers Who Walk

for Ruthie Ann Miles

Bathed in what tears?
In the tears
of mothers
who walk.

What mother does not walk?
Does not hold her child's hand,
feeling how cold
how dry
how warm.

What mother does not
give her child her own large mitten if
the smaller hand
seems colder than her own?

What mother does not expect to
cross the street with her child,
a small step up on the curb,
walking with a friend,
talking of the day
or not talking,
a stroller between them,

a brief passage
from one side to the other.

Spuyten Duyvil

for Mindy Sobota

It takes practice to view the land.
Wild onion—cardinal—bird nest—
and the exact point where the tide
becomes copper against the sea of blue.

You notice silver in the rock, and a plaque:
"Here's where the Indians sold
Manhattan for sixty guilders."

I smell the first warmth—
complicated smell of March above the city—
clay, crocus, daffodil.

Once I was a lonely scholar,
and the earth still smelled the same.
Once I was a short-necked girl,
and the earth still smelled the same.

Now we're pushing babies all the way
to Spuyten Duyvil.

One turn of the carriage and the crocuses!
After seasons of neglect—sixty guilders sold—
Will the crocuses still have us?
Will the crocuses take us back?

The Liberation Bathroom

for Elizabeth Charuvastra

You dreamed that when your children left the house
you'd turn the smallest bedroom into a
"liberation bathroom"—shrine to water.

A nurse, you wanted not to die in a hospital.
For days you didn't speak, until they brought you home;
you said "home," threw up your hands, then held your silence.

You died in a hospice bed, in your liberation bathroom,
your children holding your face.
All the forms of liberation; all the indignities of place.

Mothering as Venn Diagram

for Kathy Ruhl

That she knit me a hat to keep my head warm,
that she brought me a glass of cold water when I was sick,
even though I am old now and can carry my own water.
That her arms smell faintly of salt.

That she taught me about the Venn diagram
when I was a child seems crucial—
what are two circles that overlap,
where does one circle begin, the other end,
and what is in between?
The beautiful logic of these circles
she taught me, on a train, between one place and another.

But now what seems crucial:
the water, the yarn, the salt.

VI

Max

With thanks to Maurice Sendak

Death no wild thing
and you a boy,
Max.

One night in your room
(or body)
a forest grew

and the walls
(or cells) became
transparent

because brightness
invites
transparency, I guess.

Then a little boat
to hospital smells.
Doctors called

the forest cancer,
not obscuring leaves.
And you a boy.

You say:
"Why can't people use the word
courage

instead of something
vulgar and idiomatic
about manhood?"

Courage, I say,
is you,
Max.

In your wild suit
your small boat
and terrible forest

a man overnight—
no boy
could ever scale those walls.

You come home
and dinner is waiting,
still waiting, I hope, still warm.

*

And today my small boy
learned to swim.
He said: "The water held me, Mama.
It held me."

Old-Fashioned Rhymes for Max

I

Max, don't die.
We still have to argue
you and I
about John Berryman
whom you like
and of whom I'd wish
more wisdom
and less intelligence.

2

We take a walk around the block
to open up your lungs
and talk.

We pass the Yew Tree Antique Store
then two puppets and what's more—
the puppets are skeletons and are
playing banjos, four.

3

It hurts like hell when you sneeze
and on your torso there is a scar,
which you show me—
O bright star.

This is an automated recording from a hospital near you

for Max Ritvo

An X-ray of your soul shows
a general radiance

while the scan of your breath
shows only poetry.

We are still waiting on the biopsy
of your imagination

but we suspect it cannot be contained.

Your body cannot contain you.
You're way too wide for that.

And if there is a Jewish heaven,
it is here, on earth,
on Thirteenth Street:

you, shouting poetry
in a crowded room,
circling,
and wearing a pink kimono.

Lunch with Max on the Upper East Side

I

The skinny women on the Upper East Side
have eaten too many greens and
have come to resemble their salads.
Dry and brittle, they push kale on their plates.
They need some cooked food, and quick.

You, a young man, also skinny,
push food around on your plate—
it's warm and has the flavor of the
poison medicine the doctors give you.

2

The wildness of youth
and the wildness of death—
too much to bear, so close together.

Some loop closed by old age,
the droop of an old man's head
conferring a measure of acceptance,
head already looking at the ground, thinking:
When will a hole open up
and I'll fall into it?

3

We talk of Madame Bovary and whether her
emotions are banal and whether the doctor's are really *not* banal
and whether emotions can ever even *be* banal
or if they only *seem* banal in art.

Health does not belong to literature.
I wish it did.

Max is a poet.
Max is a poem.

We all become poems
in the end.

Marsupial Births

for Ari

I

Today we watch
a marsupial get born.

Red, tiny, covered with not-quite fur,
the small thing climbs out of its mother,
grafts itself to her,
then burrows by smell into her pouch,
there to grow.

Two births for one small kangaroo.

You, Max, waiting, in the pouch of your steamer chair,
holding your red hot-water bottle,
which you call your second Max.

2

When I gave birth I thought—oh—
death in reverse.
The pain, the pushing yourself
outside your own body,
no longer belonging to your mother,
into some other dark pouch.

So much courage to get born or die—
those giraffes dropping from the
great rooftops of their mothers' bodies—
learning to stand on the ground.

Those kangaroos—
finding their way into the dark
matted fur of their mothers' bodies.

And then the second birth—
peering out into the world.

VII

God Drank Soup from My Heart

for Sister Linda

At Sunday school Sister Linda told me that
God created us with love.
The child in me thought:
We better keep creating God with love,
as a little thank-you card to the Word made flesh.
We have to keep making it up because it made us up
and all this making up must be reciprocal.

I had a dream last night:
God drank soup from my heart
with a little ladle.
Then I drank the broth with herbs.
It went from my heart to my head,
and God drank it there.

Terrarium Sonnet

for Tony

Until I turned forty I never
saw a terrarium or knew what one was.
You led me, eyes closed, past ugly rivers
and cars and February blight

to the terrarium store where we made
one each. Domed in glass, the first peals
of spring, light green, a darker green, moss
moss moss—I wanted to inhale green light.

Cheek on moss pillow, eat the sprig, palms
in soil, resting there, charcoal under
tiny stones, sand and sediment,
making a world, or two small worlds:

your desert succulents and my woods—oh
my love, how could I forget to water.

Tertön

for Yangzom

There is a poem for you hiding in the cleft of a rock.
Water laps about its edges.
Written by no one, written just for you.

Its rhyme scheme is unimportant.
Its handwriting is weird.
It meets you where you live.

If you don't find it, no one else will.
So walk down to the water,
and put your hand in.

Two, three, one

Sometimes two things are not possible
but three are, and sometimes the third thing
is forgiveness.

Sometimes three things are not possible,
but two are, and the third thing is still forgiveness
waiting behind heavy furniture.

Sometimes people seem like things or furniture,
but they are never things or furniture.

And sometimes, after a terrible dream,
waking, one thing is possible: love.

When one thing is possible,
the numbers go away, so fast and hard,
because you can't even count the number of birds flying south,
you can't count them
at the speed they are flying.

You can make yourself so small

for Anna

You can make yourself so small:
cross your feet, pull your knees up,
       stay in bed.

You can make yourself so medium sized:
buy what others are wearing,
say what others are saying,
       go to work.

Or, you can make yourself so large:
get out of bed,
       open your throat to the snow.

The warmest room is the room with you

is a poem I never wrote you with that title.
I never wrote it because you are tired of poems
and prefer presence now, and deeds.

Deeds like:
I hung up my coat
I threw my soggy tea bag out
I mailed that box before the post office closed,
and I waited for you to come home
to eat dinner.

Soup is my preference
because it takes time to make,
is quiet when eaten,
and is almost always better warm.

You too
are warm, and often prefer quiet,
especially when circumnavigating
an island on foot.

I will never understand you
or God
but my ignorance makes neither you
nor God less beautiful.

Let this be our secret,
our little vow—
                your brown eyes lit up in the dark.

Some bureaucrat decided you should buy lace for your beloved on your thirteenth wedding anniversary

1

You hate lace curtains,
preferring to see the sky.

Down with filigree!
Instead, invite transparency.

2

My hatred for lace bras
is more prosaic—they itch my skin.

How does my nakedness become me now?
No lace, nothing to hide—
three children later, you've seen all of my body.

Once slim, then full.
Once quiet, then in all kinds of agony.

In childbirth, they say: open or die.
I opened.

Here is my body, still open, love—
still uncovered with lace.

Summer, Rhode Island

for Tony

You know what a lee is; I don't.
Behind a stone. No wind. Stop boat. A place.
Behind your back. My body. Stop the air.
Travel by stopping, full stop. Just there.

As *lee* is a small word. Sail easy.
Lee and unlee, light is hot.
Rest here, a while longer on my
belly. A lee, a dry derry, a drought.

August: marsh sounds, marsh looks, a ferry.
Look for other words—lucid, pellucid—
call a mind a pond? Call a pond a mind?
Lucid, penitent mendicants on a pond.

Words for clarity, words for light and heat,
words for charity—words for sleep.

Afterword

Most of my poems are poems of address, written to a "you" who changes and evolves. Some are occasional poems—written for occasions, or written occasionally. I am moved by the ancient tradition of poems written for people or events.

Our culture now lacks modes of direct address. We often publish our sentiments in the digital ether for a faceless group. In this generalized era, I long for the specificity of the dedication, the notion of: I wrote this for you, because of you. A *you* implies an *I*. Sometimes we write poems to ask people to fall in love with us. Sometimes we ask forgiveness. Sometimes we get forgiveness; sometimes we don't. But always a secret, lone reader is implied, as well as permission to peer in, to take part in the relation.

I remember being so worried when I read in college that the lyric "I" was in crisis. If the *I* was suspect, I thought, then was the reading *you* also suspect? Frank O'Hara reassured me when he wrote, "The poem is. . . between two persons instead of two pages."

Lewis Hyde argues, in his seminal book *The Gift,* that poetry takes place in a gift economy. When I read *The Gift,* I took this argument to heart, as well as his admonition that "a gift not given away ceases to be a gift." I am primarily a playwright, but I never stopped writing poems after I started writing plays. On some level I don't see the distinction between plays and poems. Both require extra white space on the page for some unnamed alchemy to happen, and both require a kind of singing voice. Sometimes I snatch a couplet or two and put them in my plays. My secret poems written over the years represent a quiet and secret bond—writing for individuals, or writing for myself, rather than for an audience. But my husband, and Lewis Hyde's book, encouraged me to give these poems away.

At some point, I connected with Lewis Hyde through a student, and he gave me a poem, and I hid it in my desk. I like to keep poems in a secret compartment in my desk. I am fortunate that my desk has many secret cubbies and hiding places. It is dark wood, and I inherited it from my second cousin Beulah, who never married, wore a small, neat, grey wig, and collected antique valentines, which she probably put into her secret cubbies. They are the natural hiding place of antique valentines and poems marked "Anonymous."

My Norwegian grandmother wrote verse for occasions. Her verse always rhymed and was always created with a sense of event. Event and rhyme are now a little embarrassing to poets, but my grandmother memorized poetry for oratory competitions in Iowa, and the rhymes helped her to remember.

My other poetry-writing ancestor was an Irish doctor who moved to Iowa, fought for the North in the Civil War, and was captured. He wrote scurrilous verses about his Southern captors and threw his poems out the window of the jail, to be published by the *Chicago Tribune.*

Perhaps because of my ancestors, I retain a sense of wonder about the less elevated functions of versification—celebrating occasions or getting revenge on one's captors. The function of poetry untethered from address, or occasion, or people, is less clear, though no less sublime.

A note on structure: I realize now that what separates the first three sections of this book from the last four is that I had three babies in between. Imagine three babies getting born on that blank page. And why 44 poems, and not 50 poems, or 52? Perhaps because I was 44 years old when finishing the collection, the number seemed right.

Not all of the poems in this collection have an implied occasion, but almost all of them have an implied sense of address, a *you.* I wanted to take the time to formally include you, reader, in that *you,* and to thank you for reading them.

Perhaps it's a boon that the English language does not have both a singular and a plural version of "you"; a *you* in the poem automatically opens itself to the reader. I wanted to open them to you.

Sarah Ruhl, Brooklyn, 2019

Acknowledgments

"Summer, Rhode Island" and "I wanted music" were published in *Narrative;* "I intend to give you many bowls" was in the *Los Angeles Review of Books;* "Max," "Old-Fashioned Rhymes for Max," and "This is an automated recording from a hospital near you" appeared in *Letters from Max: a book of friendship.*

A few people were instrumental in the decision to give these poems to readers beyond the original recipients. The first was my husband, who admonished me not to hoard my poems, arguing that he should not be their only reader. Most of these poems are for him, written specifically, privately, and with love, for him.

The second was my brilliant former student Max Ritvo. He persuaded me to share my poems with him and to read my poems aloud. He also gave one of my poems to the beautiful poet Elizabeth Metzger, who published my first grown-up poem in the *Los Angeles Review of Books.* To Michael Wiegers at Copper Canyon, I owe a huge debt of gratitude. And to Terry Nemeth, my gentle and wonderful publisher at Theatre Communications Group, who introduced me to Michael.

My thanks to some other crucial readers and inspirers: Jessica Thebus, Sarah Curtis, Carrie Fountain, Ari Ritvo, Eloise Fink, Mark Tardi, Craig Watson. And to Albert Lee, Bruce Ostler, Emma Feiwel, and Dorian Karchmar. To my dear ones to whom I first read many poems aloud: Kathleen Tolan, Andy Bragen, Jorge Cortiñas, and my children, Hope, Anna, and William. Great gratitude to all the living dedicatees: Sherry Mason, Mindy Sobota, Kathleen Ruhl, Kate Ruhl, Ari Ritvo, Yangzom, and Tony Charuvastra. And to all of the dedicatees who are no longer with us: Max Ritvo, Elizabeth Charuvastra, and my dad, Patrick Ruhl.

About the Author

Sarah Ruhl is a playwright, essayist, and poet. She is a MacArthur award recipient, a two-time Pulitzer Prize finalist, and a Tony award nominee. Her book of essays, *100 Essays I Don't Have Time to Write*, was published by FSG and named a notable book by the *New York Times*. Her book *Letters from Max*, coauthored with Max Ritvo and published by Milkweed, was on the *New Yorker*'s list of the best poetry of 2018. Her plays include *The Clean House; Dead Man's Cell Phone; Dear Elizabeth; Eurydice; For Peter Pan on her 70th Birthday; How to Transcend a Happy Marriage; In the Next Room, or the Vibrator Play; Late: a cowboy song; Melancholy Play; The Oldest Boy; Orlando; Passion Play; Stage Kiss;* and a translation of *Three Sisters*. Her plays have been produced on and off Broadway, around the country, and internationally, where they've been translated into over fifteen languages. Originally from Chicago, Ms. Ruhl received her MFA from Brown University, where she studied with Paula Vogel. She has received the Susan Smith Blackburn Prize, the Whiting Award, the Lilly Award, a PEN award for midcareer playwrights, the National Theatre Conference's Person of the Year award, and the Steinberg Distinguished Playwright award. You can read more about her work at www.SarahRuhlplaywright.com. She teaches at the Yale School of Drama, and she lives in Brooklyn with her family.

Poetry is vital to language and living. Since 1972, Copper Canyon Press has published extraordinary poetry from around the world to engage the imaginations and intellects of readers, writers, booksellers, librarians, teachers, students, and donors.

WE ARE GRATEFUL FOR THE MAJOR SUPPORT PROVIDED BY:

THE PAUL G. ALLEN
FAMILY FOUNDATION

Lannan

TO LEARN MORE ABOUT UNDERWRITING
COPPER CANYON PRESS TITLES,
PLEASE CALL 360-385-4925 EXT. 103

WE ARE GRATEFUL FOR THE MAJOR SUPPORT PROVIDED BY:

Anonymous

Jill Baker and Jeffrey Bishop

Anne and Geoffrey Barker

Donna and Matt Bellew

Diana Broze

John R. Cahill

The Beatrice R. and Joseph A.
  Coleman Foundation Inc.

The Currie Family Fund

Laurie and Oskar Eustis

Saramel and Austin Evans

Mimi Gardner Gates

Gull Industries Inc. on behalf of
  William True

The Trust of Warren A. Gummow

Carolyn and Robert Hedin

Bruce Kahn

Phil Kovacevich and Eric Wechsler

Lakeside Industries Inc. on behalf
  of Jeanne Marie Lee

Maureen Lee and Mark Busto

Peter Lewis

Ellie Mathews and Carl Youngmann
  as The North Press

Larry Mawby

Hank Meijer

Jack Nicholson

Petunia Charitable Fund and
  adviser Elizabeth Hebert

Gay Phinny

Suzie Rapp and Mark Hamilton

Emily and Dan Raymond

Jill and Bill Ruckelshaus

Cynthia Sears

Kim and Jeff Seely

Dan Waggoner

Randy and Joanie Woods

Barbara and Charles Wright

Caleb Young as C. Young Creative

The dedicated interns and
  faithful volunteers of
  Copper Canyon Press

The Chinese character for poetry is made up of two parts:
"word" and "temple." It also serves as pressmark for
Copper Canyon Press.

The poems are set in Adobe Caslon Pro.
Book design and composition by Phil Kovacevich.